**Genre** Realistic Fiction

 **Essential Question**
What experiences can change the way you see yourself and the world around you?

King of the Board

by Diana Noonan
illustrated by Carlos Araujo

Chapter 1
Giants in the Park 2

Chapter 2
Battle of the Kings 7

Chapter 3
My Kind of Sport 12

Respond to Reading 16

PAIRED READ All on Her Own 17

Focus on Literary Elements 20

CHAPTER 1
Giants in the Park

I hate Saturday mornings. A **transition** from calm to **chaos** takes over our house. Everything goes crazy! I live in a family of sports stars. Dad, who's a baseball **genius**, runs around looking for his glove. Mom, who's a **superb** tennis player, gets ready for an early game. My brother Adam, the fastest runner at school, packs his bag for practice.

Then my cousins call about their lost softball gear, and my grandpa starts honking the car horn out front. He drives Adam to the track on his way to the golf course.

The worst part is when everyone asks me if I want to watch their games. When it's a special game, I go to support them, but most weeks I say, "No thanks." The truth is, I get bored watching tennis or baseball. I also get hot, tired, and sore from sitting on the bleachers, listening to everyone shouting and cheering.

I can't help it. I'm just not interested in sports. I've tried everything from soccer to underwater hockey. The fact is, there is no sport that I really want to play. And there is no sport that I really want to watch.

At school everyone thinks I love sports because of my family. I let them think that because otherwise they might treat me with **disdain**. They wouldn't like me. Some people only like sporty people.

STOP AND CHECK

Why doesn't the narrator like Saturday mornings?

3

At breakfast one Saturday, Mom asked, "Clinton, why don't you meet Dad and me at the park after our games? We can have a picnic together."

"Great idea," Dad said. "We can visit that new **recreation** area. There's a golfing area."

Adam added, "The new outdoor games area is huge, too!"

Later, while I waited for my parents at the park, I checked out the new games area. Adam was right—it was huge. There was an outdoor gym and even a mini-golf course. There was also a giant checkerboard with chess pieces the size of kitchen chairs.

Two men were standing on the board, playing a game. I climbed to the top of a slide to get a bird's-eye view of them.

At first I just enjoyed watching the players haul the giant chess pieces around. Then I noticed that each piece only made certain moves. Some pieces moved from side to side, while others moved forward and back, or on a diagonal line. They looked like they were dancing.

"There you are!" called a voice below me. "We've been looking for you everywhere."

"Sorry, Mom," I called back. I looked at my watch. I had been completely **focused** on the game for more than 20 minutes without realizing it. I climbed down from the slide.

"Can we eat here?" I asked. I didn't want to miss the end of the chess game.

STOP AND CHECK

What does Clinton discover at the park?

CHAPTER 2

Battle of the Kings

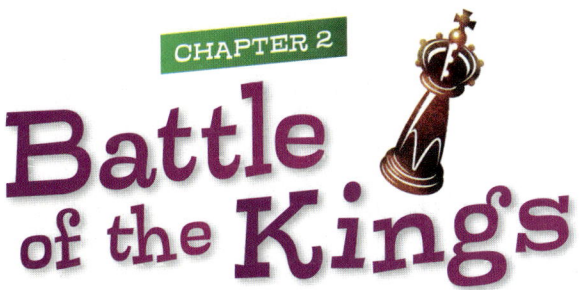

After our visit to the park, I went to the library to borrow books on chess. I also learned about it on the Internet. In fact, I became chess **obsessed**. It's all I thought about.

I don't know why I liked it so much. I'm good at math, and chess is kind of mathematical. But it was more than that. I liked the pieces, and the way they danced around each other.

I tried talking to my dad about chess, but he said that board games weren't his thing.

Grandpa felt the same. When I asked if he liked chess, he said, "Give me a set of golf clubs any day!"

I couldn't find anyone who wanted to come with me to watch chess. And I'm not allowed to go to the park alone. I thought I'd never get to see the giant pieces in action again.

Then, the next Saturday, Mom agreed to meet me at the park after her tennis game. This time, two women were playing. Mom and I sat on the park bench and watched.

The women were really nice. When they saw me watching, they explained some of the rules. I already knew most of them from my research.

After a while, I began suggesting moves to them. Mom whispered that I shouldn't interrupt, but the women didn't seem to mind. In fact, they asked me for ideas. I was surprised, and I worried that my moves were silly, but I did my best.

After they finished the game, the women asked me if I belonged to a chess club. When I told them I had never played before, they suggested that I join a club.

STOP AND CHECK

What happens when Clinton watches the chess game at the park?

The women added, "You're very **talented**, Clinton. You could be a great player. Our chess club meets on Tuesday evenings at Bay Hall. Other kids your age will be there. You should come."

"Thank you," said Mom. "That's a very kind **invitation**."

As we walked home, I asked Mom, "Can I go? Please?" I was so excited!

She replied, "Sure, if that's what you want."

That night, I had a strange dream. I was a chess piece, but I wasn't dancing on the board with the other pieces. I was fighting a battle with them!

> **STOP AND CHECK**
>
> How does Clinton help the women playing chess in the park?

CHAPTER 3

My Kind of Sport

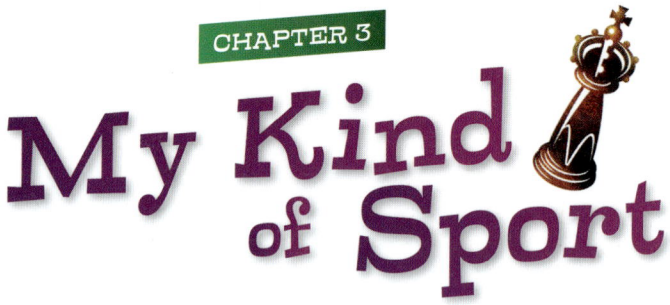

After that night at chess club, I lived for Tuesdays. Lots of kids my age came to the club, and I made some great friends. There was so much to learn about the game, and I played all through the summer and fall.

Once a month, we had a chess lesson, where one of the senior players taught us about **strategy**. We discussed the moves we might make when chess pieces were in certain positions.

The rest of the time we played each other. Players are **ranked** on what's called a grade ladder. I started at the bottom, of course, but slowly, I started moving up.

When winter arrived, chess club switched to Saturday mornings. Suddenly I was part of my family's crazy Saturday **routine** of getting out of the house on time.

"Where's my notebook? Where's my jacket?" I shouted. It was fun to be part of the craziness, but I still felt different. I knew my family didn't understand why I wanted to play chess instead of football.

At the end of winter, my club held its annual tournament. I didn't think there was any **prospect** of my whole family coming. I expected only Mom and Dad to be there. Chess can be kind of slow, and unless you love it, it's not much fun to watch.

STOP AND CHECK

What happens at Clinton's chess club?

13

So it was a real surprise when everybody showed up to support me: Mom, Dad, Adam, Grandpa, my uncle and aunt, and even a few cousins came, too!

The games lasted all day, but all my family stayed the whole time. Some of my cousins were playing computer games by the end. I didn't blame them, because I knew how bored I got when I watched sports.

I played my best, but to be honest, I didn't care about winning. Just being there and playing chess was the important thing.

I didn't win the junior section trophy, but I did win an award for Most Promising Player. For a moment, my family looked stunned. Then they went wild! They acted like I had hit a home run at a baseball game.

After we got home, Dad came up to my room. I was hanging my award on the wall. Dad handed me a box.

He said, "I always dreamed of buying you your first baseball glove," he said. "Now I think this is the best present I can give you."

I opened the box and found a beautiful wooden chess set. Dad gave me a giant hug and said, "I'm so proud of you, Clinton. You've found your sport."

"Thanks, Dad!" I said. I knew that he was seeing me from a whole new **perspective**. And I was seeing myself in a new way, too.

STOP AND CHECK

Why was Clinton happy even though he didn't win the chess tournament?

Summarize

Summarize the important events in *King of the Board*. Use the graphic organizer to help you list key details.

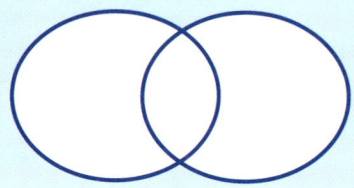

Text Evidence

1. Compare Clinton's experiences of watching baseball or tennis with how he feels watching chess in the park. **COMPARE AND CONTRAST**

2. Look at the word *blame* on page 14. What clues help you to figure out what the word means? **VOCABULARY**

3. What is it like at Clinton's house on a typical Saturday morning? Compare this to a chess club meeting. Write about how the two settings affect Clinton differently. **WRITE ABOUT READING**

CCSS **Genre** Realistic Fiction

Compare Texts
Read about what changed a girl's belief in herself.

ALL ON HER OWN

Sophie Larson signed up for junior baseball. She knew she could count on Gramps to help her play well because Gramps had been a baseball coach.

Training with Gramps was hard work. "Can't we take a few days off?" Sophie asked. "I've been practicing every day."

"Do you want to be an okay player or a great player?" asked Gramps.

Sophie sighed, then grabbed her glove and bat before following Gramps outside.

17

For the rest of the pre-season, Gramps taught Sophie all about the game. Sometimes Sophie had doubts about being good enough, but those doubts disappeared when she was with Gramps.

On the morning of her first game, Gramps and Sophie checked out the baseball field. The outfield fence looked so far away. The trees beyond the fence seemed to whisper to Sophie, "Can you hit this far?"

Sophie said, "Please stand where I can see you, Gramps. I can play well as long as you're there."

That afternoon, Sophie looked for Gramps when she stepped up to the plate, but he was nowhere to be seen. There was no time left. Sophie had to face the pitcher.

Sophie swung the bat. *Slam!* The ball was in the air, and Sophie took off for first base, then second base, then a slide into third base. Her teammates leaped to their feet, yelling. Then the next batter hit Sophie home. As she crossed the plate, she saw Gramps standing there cheering with everyone else.

Sophie rushed to him and asked, "Where were you, Gramps? I needed you!"

"You only thought you needed me," said Gramps. "When you face a pitcher, you're on your own. Now you know you can do it, with or without me."

Sophie nodded. "You're right, Gramps. I can do it on my own. Next time, I'll hit it out of the park!"

Make Connections

What convinced Sophie she was a good baseball player in *All on Her Own*? ESSENTIAL QUESTION

Compare the experiences that changed how Clinton and Sophie saw themselves. How are they similar? How are they different? TEXT TO TEXT

Focus on Literary Elements

Figurative Language A metaphor is a kind of figurative language. It compares two things that are not alike. Personification is another kind of figurative language. It gives an object the qualities of a living person.

Read and Find In *King of the Board*, Clinton climbs on a slide to have a "bird's-eye view" (page 5). This metaphor compares Clinton's view with the view a bird might have.

In *All on Her Own*, the author uses personification when the trees "whisper" (page 18). Turn to page 7 in *King of the Board*. Find another example of personification in the second paragraph..

Your Turn

Choose one of the examples of figurative language in Read and Find. Reread the text. Then draw a picture that shows what that example might look like if it were real. Share your drawing with your group.